Will it sin

Written by Clare Helen Welsh
Photographed by Will Amlot

Collins

Zac has a shell.

Will it sink?

Yes, the shell sinks.

Will this sink?

Yes, the fox sinks.

Will this sink?

Yes, the van sinks.

Will this sink?

No.

The cup will not sink.

The cup fills ...

and then sinks!

/w/

14

/y/

15

After reading

Letters and Sounds: Phase 3

Word count: 40

Focus phonemes: /w/ /y/ /z/ /x/ /v/ /nk/ /th/ /sh/

Common exception words: the, no, and

Curriculum links: Understanding the World: The World

Early learning goals: Reading: use phonic knowledge to decode regular words and read them aloud accurately; demonstrate understanding when talking with others about what they have read

Developing fluency

- Discuss the features of non-fiction texts such as photographs, labels and captions.
- Look at the question marks used in the book. Explain these are used when someone asks something.
- Take turns to read pages of the book with your child.

Phonic practice

- Look through the book with your child and ask them to find a word with the /x/ sound in it (*fox*)
- Can your child think of any words that rhyme with **sink**? (e.g. *pink, think, wink, link, clink, blink*) These words all end in the /nk/ sound.
- Look at the "I spy sounds" pages (14–15). Discuss the picture with your child. Can they find items/ examples of words with the /w/ sound or the /y/ sound? (*water bottle, whale, wheels, wool, watch, whistle, yellow, yo-yo, yarn*)

Extending vocabulary

- Ask your child:
  - What is the opposite of sink? (*float*)
  - The children are doing an experiment. What other words could we use that mean experiment? (e.g. *test, investigation*)